STEM IN THE SUMMER OLYMPICS
THE SCIENCE BEHIND
BASKETBALL

by Jenny Fretland VanVoorst

po go

Ideas for Parents and Teachers

Pogo Books let children practice reading informational text while introducing them to nonfiction features such as headings, labels, sidebars, maps, and diagrams, as well as a table of contents, glossary, and index.

Carefully leveled text with a strong photo match offers early fluent readers the support they need to succeed.

Before Reading

- "Walk" through the book and point out the various nonfiction features. Ask the student what purpose each feature serves.
- Look at the glossary together. Read and discuss the words.

Read the Book

- Have the child read the book independently.
- Invite him or her to list questions that arise from reading.

After Reading

- Discuss the child's questions. Talk about how he or she might find answers to those questions.
- Prompt the child to think more. Ask: When a ball hits the ground, some of its kinetic energy is changed into a sound. Can you think of other sounds that might come from kinetic energy?

Pogo Books are published by Jump!
5357 Penn Avenue South
Minneapolis, MN 55419
www.jumplibrary.com

Copyright © 2020 Jump!
International copyright reserved in all countries.
No part of this book may be reproduced in any form without written permission from the publisher.

Library of Congress Cataloging-in-Publication Data

Names: Fretland VanVoorst, Jenny, 1972- author.
Title: The science behind basketball / by Jenny Fretland VanVoorst.
Description: Minneapolis, MN: Pogo Books, published by Jump!, Inc., [2020]
Series: STEM in the Summer Olympics
Includes bibliographical references and index.
Audience: 7 to 10.
Identifiers: LCCN 2019001225 (print)
LCCN 2019004691 (ebook)
ISBN 9781641289016 (ebook)
ISBN 9781641288996 (hardcover: alk. paper)
Subjects: LCSH: Basketball—Juvenile literature.
Sports sciences—Juvenile literature.
Classification: LCC GV885.1 (ebook)
LCC GV885.1 .F74 2020 (print) | DDC 796.323—dc23
LC record available at https://lccn.loc.gov/2019001225

Editor: Susanne Bushman
Designer: Michelle Sonnek

Photo Credits: mihalec/Shutterstock, cover (clipboard); Cherdchai charasri/Shutterstock, cover (basketball); Action Plus Sports Images/Alamy, 1; Geraldo Bubniak/ZUMA Wire/Alamy, 3; Foto Arena LTDA/Alamy, 4, 20-21; Mark Reis/Colorado Springs Gazette/TNS/Alamy, 5; CP DC Press/Shutterstock, 6-7, 12-13, 17, 23; ZUMA Press, Inc./Alamy, 8-9; Leonard Zhukovsky/Shutterstock, 10, 14-15; Kyodo/Newscom, 11; Pertusinas/Shutterstock, 16; Koji Aoki/AFLO SPORT/Alamy, 18-19.

Printed in the United States of America at Corporate Graphics in North Mankato, Minnesota.

TABLE OF CONTENTS

CHAPTER 1

DRIBBLE, PASS, SHOOT!

Basketball players run. They pass. They shoot! This sport is action-packed!

Olympians are the best in the game. They are strong and fast. But they also use **physics** to go for gold!

The Olympian looks left and then right. Where can she pass? A basketball has **potential energy** when a player is holding it. This is stored energy. It is based on an object's location.

When the player passes, **dribbles**, or shoots the ball, it has **kinetic energy**. This is the energy of an object in motion.

Basketball games are noisy. Shoes screech. Balls thud. What causes these noises? Energy changing form. Kinetic energy becomes sound. Like when a ball bounces or when a player's shoes screech. This happens when players stop. It also happens as they change directions.

DID YOU KNOW?

Some bounces produce louder sounds. Why? There is more energy in the bounce!

CHAPTER 2

....

BASKETBALLS IN MOTION

He shoots! The ball flies straight toward the net. Why? A moving object moves in one direction. Unless it is acted on by a **force**. This is a **law of motion**.

This player blocks the ball! She acts as a force. She changes the ball's path.

The ball hits the **backboard**. The backboard stops it from moving in its original direction. The ball changes paths again. It bounces into the net! She scores!

backboard

A player dribbles. He pushes the ball down to the floor. It bounces back up. Why? When force is applied to an object, the object returns the force. The floor returns the force of the player's push. The ball moves back to the player's hand.

DID YOU KNOW?

Balls bounce at different heights. It depends on force. Balls that bounce higher hit the floor with greater force. The force the floor responds with is also greater.

CHAPTER 3
SLOWING DOWN

Friction slows objects down. This happens any time two objects touch. When more surface area of the objects touch, the greater the friction. See the basketball's bumps? This is called **pebbling**.

pebbling · · · · · ▶

Pebbling creates more surface area. This makes more friction during bounces. The bounces are slower. Without pebbling, it would be hard to control the ball.

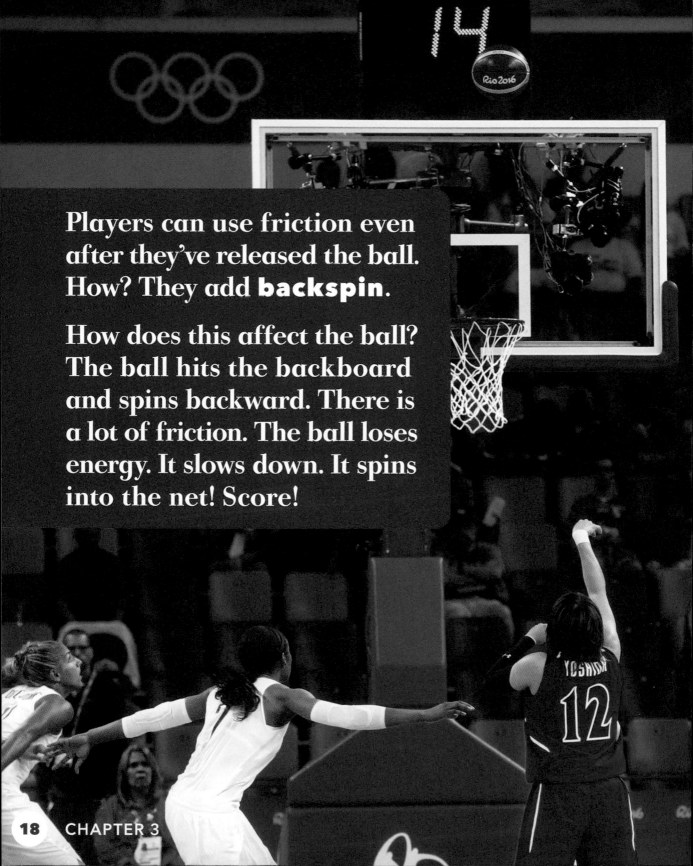

Players can use friction even after they've released the ball. How? They add **backspin**.

How does this affect the ball? The ball hits the backboard and spins backward. There is a lot of friction. The ball loses energy. It slows down. It spins into the net! Score!

TAKE A LOOK!

How does a player add backspin? Take a look!

① **The player bends his or her wrist back.**

② **The player snaps his or her wrist down and forward during release.**

③ **The ball rotates backward. It continues to spin as it flies.**

There are 10 seconds left! This Olympian fakes left, then goes right. **Traction** helps. This is friction between a shoe and the ground. Without traction, players' feet would slide. Basketball shoes allow the right amount of traction.

Basketball is physics in action! How do you use physics to play?

DID YOU KNOW?

Shoe designers make shoe soles for different floors. Basketball shoe soles have special designs. Why? Players change directions so often!

ACTIVITIES & TOOLS

TRY THIS!

UNDER PRESSURE

What's inside a basketball? Air! Look at the effect air pressure has on a ball's bounce with this activity.

What You Need:
- three basketballs:
  - one inflated to the proper pressure
  - one slightly underinflated
  - one slightly overinflated
- a measuring stick
- a friend

❶ On a flat spot, hold one of the basketballs in your hands and extend your arms straight out in front of your body, parallel to the floor or ground.

❷ Drop the ball.

❸ Ask your friend to use the measuring stick to measure how high the ball bounces.

❹ Record the height.

❺ Repeat steps one through four two more times.

❻ Repeat with the other two balls.

❼ Now look at your data. Add each basketball's measurements together and then divide by three. This is the average bounce height for each ball.

❽ Compare the average heights. Are you surprised by the results? Why or why not?

GLOSSARY

backboard: The upright board behind the basketball hoop.

backspin: A throwing technique that causes a basketball to rotate backward as it flies through the air.

dribbles: Bounces a ball continuously.

force: An action that produces, stops, or changes the shape of a movement or object.

friction: The force that slows down objects when they rub against each other.

kinetic energy: The energy of motion.

law of motion: One of the three laws of physics that govern moving objects, such as every action has an equal and opposite reaction, that was discovered by Isaac Newton.

pebbling: The small bumpy grain on the surface of a basketball that allows for greater surface area and greater friction.

physics: The science that deals with matter, energy, and their interactions.

potential energy: Stored energy that can be released to turn into kinetic energy.

traction: The force that keeps a moving body from slipping on a surface.

INDEX

TO LEARN MORE

Finding more information is as easy as 1, 2, 3.

❶ **Go to www.factsurfer.com**

❷ **Enter "sciencebehindbasketball" into the search box.**

❸ **Choose your book to see a list of websites.**

FACT
SURFER